The Quick and Dirty Guide to Starting Your Business!

By Deirdre Haynes, Ed.S, LPCS, NCC, DCC

© 2018 Deirdre F. Haynes. All rights reserved worldwide.

This publication is protected under the US Copyright Act of 1976 and all other applicable international, federal, state, and local laws. No part of this work may be reproduced, distributed, or transmitted in any form or by any means, without the prior written permission of the author.
In the case of brief quotations embodied in critical reviews and certain other noncommercial uses permitted by copyright laws, excerpts from the text may be used. It is requested in these instances to include credit to the author and if possible, a link to www.theblindspotbiz.com.

For permission requests, please contact the author directly at:
support@theblindspotbiz.com

Dear Reader,

If you build it, they will come. This is the mantra I chanted to myself as I started my service-based mental health practice (www.dhaynestherapy.com) and my online self-help store (www.theblindspotbiz.com). This has proven to be a true statement since someone is always looking for your products or services. The key is that you have to get out of your own way in order to create the products or services they are itching to buy.

I know. I know. It is much easier said than done. Yes, it may get hard at times, but I truly believe that when you set your mind to accomplishing something…by any means necessary….it will come to fruition. The problem is that so many people give up before they even start! They listen and believe their inner critic that tells them that no one will want what they have to offer, that people will laugh at their products, and that no one will buy their products or services because they are just a _____ (fill in the blank). That same inner critic keeps asking, "Who are you to think that you can become an entrepreneur?" All of those negative voices have kept many people from sharing their gifts with the world and living the life of their dreams. I know this is happening because those same voices were on repeat in my head as well. **However, despite the voices, I JUMPED!**

I wrote this book for people that are tired of playing games with themselves and listening to their inner critic. Those people that have said they were starting their business for years but have not made any efforts to actually do it. If this sounds like you then this book is the **blueprint** you need to get started.

Please note: *This book is not a comprehensive guide on how to open every type of business imaginable. It is not possible for me to cover* **ALL** *the nuances that could occur when starting a product or service-based business.* **Instead this book provides a quick and dirty outline of the fundamental components and essential elements needed when starting a business.**

So, are you ready to stop playing and to begin the journey to entrepreneurship? If so, let's begin……

Sincerely,

Deirdre F. Haynes, Ed.S, LPCS, NCC, DCC

Chapters

Part 1: My Entrepreneurial Story
- 1.1. Creative People Must Create!
- 1.2. Deirdre Haynes Counseling Services
- 1.3. The Deirdre Haynes Experience
- 1.4. The Blindspot Biz
- 1.5. Go With The Flow

Part 2: What is Your Why?
- 2.1 What is Your Why?
- 2.2 What Lights You Up?
- 2.3 Your Gifts
- 2.4 We Are Here To Serve

Part 3: Your Ideal Client
- 3.1 Your Ideal Client
- 3.2 Profile Your Ideal Client
- 3.3 The Client Experience

Part 4: Business Essentials
- 4.1 Business Essentials
- 4.2 Intentional vs. Unintentional Entrepreneur
- 4.3 Research and Development
- 4.4 A Word About Sacrifices
- 4.5 Branding Your Business
- 4.6 Business License vs Retail License
- 4.7 Business Location
- 4.8 Business Forms
- 4.9 It's Time To Get Paid!

Part 5: Professionalism
- 5.1 Professionalism
- 5.2 The ____ Experience

    5.3   Have Your Stuff Together
    5.4   Under Promise and Over Deliver
    5.5   Be On Time
    5.6   Be Honest and Transparent

Part 6: Marketing your Business
    6.1   Marketing Your Business
    6.2   Historical Marketing
    6.3   Innovative Marketing

Part 1:

My Entrepreneurial Story

1.1 Creative People Must Create!

My entrepreneurial journey began accidently. I was a school counselor in Marion, SC at the time because I had moved from Columbia, SC for a change of pace. I didn't know anyone in Florence, SC, which is where I was living, and I was off for summer break. Out of pure boredom, I began watching a craft show on HGTV called That's Clever! On the show, I saw people making all kinds of things from clay, wire, and other odds and ends. It seemed like a neat thing to do but my interest really peaked when I saw a lady make really cool earrings using beads, clay and wire. It looked so easy to make that I decided to visit my Hobby Lobby store that same day.

Hobby Lobby was a wonderland of all kinds of craft materials and beautiful odds and ends. I settled on some eclectic beads and wire that could be shaped to form eyepin earrings. These are earrings that are created by simply putting beads on the eyepin (straight wire) and then using an earring hook to attach it to your ear. I rushed home to "play" with these materials and soon found that I had created some cute eyepin earrings. That was easy enough to create, so I decided to step it up a notch.

After a couple of days of playing around with some wire, I made a hoop earring that was actually sturdy and quite cute! I was proud of myself and felt accomplished. My only thought at that time was to make myself some really stylish, beaded earrings instead of paying $7-$10 for the same earrings in department stores. Score!

When school started, I reported to school like usual. As I was walking up the hall on my lunch break, I stuck my head in one of my favorite colleague's classroom and held up a pair of hoop earrings I made. As soon as I did that, students in the classroom as well as the teacher asked me how much I was selling them for and said that they wanted one. Eureka! The lightbulb went off! I had never once considered selling my goods. To me, this was just a hobby to counter the boring summer days at home while my son was at summer camp!

After that moment, almost all the teachers in the school started placing orders for earrings, then bracelets, then necklaces. I did not know how to create those pieces of jewelry but their desire for them pushed me to research and come up with a way to "**supply the demand**." During the major holidays like Mother's Day, Father's Day, Christmas, Valentines, Easter, etc. I racked up orders. Soon, family members of the staff were putting in orders as well.

Eventually, I began to sell my jewelry at the local flea market. By then, I had moved up to selling jewelry made from real stones such as tiger eye, turquoise and even hematite. I included the properties associated with these stones as a form of marketing. For instance, hematite is said to decrease stress and anxiety levels.

My customers began asking if I made any homemade lotions, bath and body products, or candles. I told them to give me two weeks and I would have some. Sure enough, I went to Hobby Lobby bought the books and products to make soaps, soy candles, body lotions, bath salts, and body oils. In two weeks, I was selling those products. I realized then that my customers steered the various directions my business was moving in and they also stretched me in ways that made me do things I never thought I could do!

The more business I received the more professional I wanted my products to look. I created professional-looking labels and tags for my products. I also began to package my products in gorgeous and ornate baskets that made a wonderful impression on my customers. Who doesn't like to get a beautiful basket with lots of goodies and sparkly ribbons? Soon, a local floral shop started selling my baskets during the major holidays! I was tired, but I was loving life and making good money!

I continued making and selling my jewelry and body products when I initially returned to my hometown in Columbia, SC. Eventually, my time grew scarce and even though I would literally "zone out" into a space of pure creative energy when creating my beloved products, I had to discontinue making them. I made lots of supplemental money and gained many loyal customers selling my wares, but I had to focus on my career.

1. 2 Deirdre Haynes Counseling Services

Once I began to feel bored with my school counseling position and began to desire some excitement in my life, I stumbled into my private mental health practice. One day, I wondered aloud if I could open up a private practice. I decided to research to figure out what needed to be done to make this happen.

I already had my Master's and Education Specialist degrees in Secondary School Counseling and K-12 School Counseling. I also had obtained one of the highest honors any teacher can obtain which is to become a National Board-Certified Teacher. This certification provided me with a $13,000 bonus for 10 years. I was happy, comfortable, but still unfulfilled. I wanted more.

So, I completed the licensure application, got approved to test, passed the test on the first go, and began my Licensed Professional Counselor Internship. Two years later I was certified to practice and three years after that I started the process to become a Licensed Professional Counselor Supervisor.

Initially, I was not sure if I wanted to work part-time for a counseling facility for even more money or if I wanted to branch out on my own. However, once I started the process, I knew that I had to see if I could really do it.

Once, I had the LPC license, I began to look for a location. I had been told that opening a mental health practice was one of the easiest businesses to open because all you really needed was a chair for the client, a chair for yourself and some privacy. That sounded easy enough.

1.3 The Deirdre Haynes Experience

I quickly found a small office space in an ideal part of town for an unbelievably low price! It was meant to be. I set out to decorate my office and set-up shop for my clients. I tend to be quite OCD (Obsessive Compulsive Disorder) with my attention to detail so acting as if I was the client came easy. I played out in my mind, step-by-step, how clients would experience me from start to finish. Something I like to call the Deirdre Haynes Experience.

I know that I like high quality things that tend to be on the expensive side, so I envisioned my perfect client being the exact same way. Everything I ordered or created for my office was based on how my ideal client would view it. Looking back now I have to smile because so many clients have praised me on how professional and well-done my office, website, procedures and systems are and how much they appreciate the forethought I put into creating an experience that is easy and relaxed. Creating an easy, relaxed and high-quality experience was and still is my primary desire.

1.4 The Blindspot Biz

The Blindspot Biz caught me by surprise! I was racking my brain to figure out how I could sell my books through my counseling practice. No matter how I tried, I could not make it make sense. One day in October 2017, I had an epiphany that took me by surprise. I was not making any progress in figuring out a way to market my books and other products through my counseling practice because my private counseling practice was a service-based business and to sell my books, courses, and worksheets I would need to create a product-based business. These are two very different business models. Eureka Again!

That morning, I began to form my new business. By 6 pm, I not only had the name for my new business, but I also had the logo completed and my 2nd website was being created!!! I chose the name, The Blindspot Biz, because my business mission is to target the blindspots in people's lives. Blindspots are those areas that are dysfunctional in some way, but they are not easily seen. Blindspots are those things that lie just around the corner, that you know are there, but you can't quite put your finger on what it is.

My business goal was and still is to illuminate those blindspot areas by helping people become aware that they exist, then by helping them work to change the mindset that is keeping them stuck which will eventually transform their lives. That is the underlying mission for every product or service I create.

1.5 Go With The Flow

When it is time, it is time, and nothing can stop things from happening! Admittedly, the Blindspot Biz was developed blindingly fast and has proven to be a formidable opponent. The learning curve is steep since I have never done many of things that are required to start and maintain an online business, however, instead of feeling defeated I continue to look at it like an awesome opportunity to grow. I have indeed grown in ways that I never imagined all because I decided to feel the fear and jump anyway. That is true courage and I hope that after reading my story and this book, you decide to jump into your own destiny!

Part 2:

WHAT IS YOUR WHY?

2.1 What Is Your Why?

What is your why? Why are you even thinking of starting a business? If your sole reason for creating a business is grounded in your desire to simply make more money, then my advice to you is to dig deeper.

People often make the mistake of chasing the money when starting a new job or business. Some people will even take on a job or career that they hate just for the money. The sad truth is that they soon find that even with the monetary increase, they are still very unhappy. This is why I always advise people to create a business around the things that they enjoy doing and/or the things that light them up.

2.2 What Lights You Up?

What are those things that you do well without even thinking about it? What are those things that you can lose yourself in that causes time to stand still until your come out of your zone several hours later feeling tired but oh so satisfied? What is that thing that you do just because you like to do it and it brings you immense pleasure?

Once you answer those questions, DO THAT THING! That is your gift and the world is waiting to receive it from you!

2.3 Your Gifts

I have a dear friend, who I will not name because I am protecting the innocent, that constantly talks about ways to save and grow your money. She has endured experiences in life that caused her to be very mindful of what she did with her money, so she began to read books on how to save and/or invest your money. She constantly discusses tools, tactics, and tidbits about things she is doing to grow her money. To her, it is just something that she likes to read about. No big deal.

Well it is a big deal! I personally don't enjoy reading about how to save and invest money. Now don't get me wrong, it is a great subject to learn about but if I have the option of reading a book about how to work with people who have experienced trauma versus a book that discusses how to invest in the stock market, you already know which one I'm going to choose.

The reason is simple. Learning about money lights her up and learning about trauma lights me up. It is our THING.

So, when she discussed with me the "fact" that she wasn't creative and didn't have a creative outlet, I was dumbfounded! Once I picked my jaw up off of the floor, I reminded her of all the lengthy conversations we had about money. I told her that those discussion weren't normal, but it was nothing special to her. I discussed with her the fact that in my spare time, I don't watch shows about money, read books on money or actually try out various techniques to see what was more effective in saving me money than the other! I simply spend money and saved money in a regular ol' account. That's it. She laughed and told me she never thought of it that way.

This is how most people operate. They do something so easily that they assume that everyone else is doing it as well. This thought pattern couldn't be further from the truth. **NO,** everyone is NOT doing the things that you do so easily and if they are then they are still not doing it the way YOU do it. That is because our gifts are as unique as we are.

2.4   We Are Here To Serve

In my opinion, our gifts were given to us to help serve others. In the big scope of things that is why we are here experiencing life at this particular time. Plain and simple. Every single job, directly or indirectly, affects other human beings. This is why no job is unnecessary. From the janitor to the CEO, they all help people in some way.

This is why I said that when considering your why you must dig deeper than the idea of simply having more money. **You are here to serve others**. How will you do that? How will the business you desire to create change the world or improve the lives of others in some way?

If your business focus is based on bringing in the most money, then the business has already failed. People will soon figure out that you only care about making a dollar by any means necessary. This means that you could potentially participate in shady, under the table deals or deliver low-quality products for a premium price simply to make a buck. Either way, your business will soon fail because word of mouth is the ultimate tool that can make or break your business.

People know when they have been bamboozled. If they believe that you are trying to get over on them then they will stop patronizing your business and stop everyone they know from patronizing your business as well. This is a slippery slope you do not want to slide down.

So, take your time and really figure out your why. Discover why your business needs to be created in order to help someone else. Don't worry! I know you have to eat too but trust me when I say that the money will come in full force once you focus your efforts on serving the needs of others.

Part 3:

YOUR IDEAL CLIENT

3.1 Your Ideal Client

Your ideal client or your ideal client avatar is the person that you wish would buy your products or utilize your services. Who this person is will vary based on the type of business you have.

Do you want a client that has issues with her children to utilize your youth counseling program? Do you want a man that loves to wear quality suits to visit your store? Do you want a working mom to buy your bath products to relax after a long day on the job and dealing with her kids? Do you want kids to create the latest sensation with a gadget or toy that you created? Do you want someone over the age of 65 to utilize your herbal vitamins that promises to give them renewed strength, energy and vitality?

Who do you want to buy your goods and services? This question is of the utmost importance as you create the foundation of your business. You have to know who your products or services will target in order to build your business around their needs and desires.

If you do this effectively, you will easily and effortlessly draw them in because you will be speaking their language!

Take a look at a recent purchase you made. Why did you buy it? Usually it was something about it that appealed to you and your particular problem. When I see ads that address working more effectively or promise to teach me about how to be a better writer, I tend to jump on them. Why? Because they know who their ideal client is, and they have worded their ad to get the attention of those needing their services. If you are not a writer or you don't work, then those ads will not peak your interest because they do not apply to you.

3.2 Profile Your Ideal Client

Take a moment to flesh out your ideal client. I promise you that completing this task will put you light years ahead of your competition.

Answer the following questions:

1. What is your ideal client's name?
2. How old is your ideal client?
3. What does your ideal client look like?
4. Where does your ideal client work?
5. How much money does your ideal client make a year?
6. If he/she is out of work, what is the reason for this?
7. What is the race and gender of your ideal client?
8. Is your ideal client married, single, partnered, divorced, widowed or separated?
9. Does your ideal client have children?
10. Where does your ideal client live?
11. What kind of vehicle does your ideal client drive?
12. What is your ideal client's highest educational level?
13. What is the religious belief, if any, of our ideal client?
14. Where does your ideal client shop?
15. What kind of magazines or books does your ideal client purchase?
16. Where does your ideal client shop for groceries, clothes, shoes, makeup, etc.?
17. What is missing from your ideal client's life?
18. Why does he/she need your product or service?
19. How will your ideal client learn about your products or services?
20. What does your ideal client spending habits and what do they splurge on?

3.3 The Client Experience

As we start to discuss the nuts and bolts of starting your own business, please keep in the forefront of your mind the ideal client avatar that you just created. Imagine that your ideal client is looking for what you have to offer right now, because they are, and you are tailoring your business around their specific needs. You should desire to impress them with your products or services from start to finish. This will make you stand out from the other people that may have a product similar to yours.

As I stated earlier, when I began the process of creating both of my businesses, I created ideal client avatars. Through the creation process, I imagined that my ideal client was providing input as to what they would like to see and/or receive as a result of utilizing my products or services. This has been most effective in attracting the very people that I desired to serve.

Imagine your ideal client wandering into your business, past your booth at the flea market, or visiting your website online. What will be their thoughts? Are the colors on your website too loud and unprofessional? Is your flea market booth dirty and unorganized? Or on the other hand, is your office relaxing and comfortable with soothing music playing in the background? Are your items easy to find on their own or must they have assistance to hunt for a specific product? How do you want your ideal client to experience you?

As you set up your business, use the client experience visual to predict your ideal client's questions and to provide a solution to their problems before they even know they have a problem in the first place. They will thank you for your effort and professionalism!

Part 4:

Business Essentials

4.1 Business Essentials

This is where the hard work and the fun begins! In this section and in the following sections, we will be exploring some of the foundational business essentials that should be considered and addressed when starting your business.

So, what do you need to know and do to get started building your business? I'm glad you asked. Let's begin....

4.2 Intentional vs. Unintentional Entrepreneur

Usually businesses start as either a hobby or as a result of someone leaving a job with a particular skill set.

The hobbyist may have an innate desire to create, collect, or study something that over time they slowly begin to master. The hobbyist becomes an **unintentional entrepreneur** when people begin to notice their wares/creations and start asking the hobbyist to sell the item to them.

If you are a hobbyist, then you will be creating a **product-based business.** Product-based businesses sell products. Simple enough, right? An example of a product-based business is my online self-help store, The Blindspot Biz. I sell my books, online courses, and merchandise through that business.

The **intentional entrepreneur** is usually a person that has a particular skill set such as cooking, accounting, dress-making, counseling, etc. that has decided to leave their 9-to-5 job for the freedom of entrepreneurship. These individuals have qualifications (or a skill set) due to their educational pursuits or on-the-job training that allow them to fulfill the needs of individuals.

If you are leaving a 9-to5 job with a particular skill-set that you plan to utilize in your business, then you are preparing to create a **service-based business**. Service-based businesses provide services to others. An example of a service-based business is my mental health practice, Deirdre Haynes Counseling Services.

Before you make the leap into entrepreneurship, it is important to ensure that you have the right qualifications especially if you are an intentional entrepreneur. When I opened my private mental health practice, I had to ensure that I was licensed to provide the services I was promoting to the public. If you are a hobbyist, then you may not need any other qualifications other than your gift and expertise in creating what you create. Either way, check with your licensing board and/or with your small business office to ensure that you have everything you need to qualify to open your business **BEFORE** you open your business.

4.3 Research and Development (R&D)

There is a term that many people in the business world use and that is Research and Development (or R&D). This is an important concept because you need to do some research into the area that you are considering entering when you start your business.

The reason for the research and development phase is to figure out if there is a need for your product. If you are a hobbyist, then you may already have a booming clientele. If you work for another business and you are leaving that business to branch out on your own, then you may already have an idea as to how high the demand is for the services you plan to offer.

Even if your clientele is great and you know that there is a demand for your services based on the business you are leaving, you still need to research the niche. I say this because moving from a side hustle to a full-time business are two very different things.

Also, family, friends, and co-workers will not pay all your bills all the time. So, you have to build clientele outside of your comfort zone if you plan to make the kind of money that pays all your bills and provides the lifestyle of your dreams.

You can research your market by doing simple Google searches to see if that product or service is prevalent in your city or not. You can also pay researchers to gather this information for you.

If your business area is gutted or full of other businesses like yours, it may be intimidating to start your business. My advice is to start it anyway because **no one can do what you do the way that you do it.**

If Rihanna was intimidated by the vice-like grip that Kylie Jenner has on the beauty industry, then we would have never been able to purchase her awesome highlighter! They are two different people with two very different personalities in the same market. Some will gravitate to Rihanna while others will gravitate to Kylie. Still others will gravitate to both depending on their favorite product. There is enough money to go around for everyone so don't allow someone else's success to keep you from starting your business. *There is enough for everyone!*

On the flip side, if your business niche is nonexistent or barely tapped into, my advice would be to do it anyway. Be cautious because the lack of businesses in that niche could be due to the fact that there simply isn't a demand for the product or service to sustain a business.

However, it could also mean that the world is waiting for you to show them that this is something that they need. Once you create the product or advertise the service the demand could be outrageous, and you may be an overnight millionaire and success story because you decided to at least try.

Just for informational purposes, the development part of R&D focuses on the creation and continuous improvements of your product and/or services.

4.4 A Word About Sacrifices

Now, that you have figured out your why, identified your ideal client and figured out if you are starting a product-based or service-based business, I need to take a moment to talk about the word: **Sacrifice**.

At its core, the word sacrifice means to give something up. When we think of giving something up most of us perceive that as a loss. In essence it is a loss, but I like to think that you are taking a loss in order to gain something else. Something greater.

If you are truly serious about starting your business, please understand right now that you will be making sacrifices. What you will sacrifice will vary based on your business but two main areas that I can guarantee will experience sacrifices, despite your business model, will be your time and your money.

Time: As an entrepreneur, you will be pulled in many areas sometimes all at once. Since you are only one, superhero-like, individual, no matter how hard you try you will not be able to do everything for everyone and still run a successful business.

Just as you got out of your bed at 6:00 am to work for someone else, you may have to get out of bed at 4:00 am to work for yourself. This is exactly what I am doing right now! Would I prefer to sleep in a little while longer in my cozy bed? Of course, I would! However, your dreams don't work unless you do!

So, before you open your business you will have to count up the cost of what it will take to run your business. Successful entrepreneurs get very comfortable with the sacrifice of time. They know that if they stay up late or get up very early in the morning those consistent sacrifices will ultimately result in pushing them ahead of their competition.

Your efforts may not be rewarded immediately. It may take months or even years for you to live the life of your dreams, but your continuous, consistent efforts will pay off.

If you prefer quick, short term rewards then starting your business may not be for you. Will there be some short-term rewards? Yes. You may get paid a little every day by happy customers even if it is not the amount of money you hoped to make that day. Someone may thank you and be incredibly grateful for how much you helped them. These are the small but meaningful rewards that can help you to keep going when times are tough.

However, that long-term vision is a monster! Just imagine yourself plugging away daily for months and even years, honing your craft, and then one day something clicks, and you are selling your products or services like crazy! This is generally how it happens. When you see successful people doing what you want to do take a moment and ask them how long they have been doing what they do. Not just how long they have been in business, but how long have they been honing their craft or skills. I can almost guarantee that it has taken years for them to get to where they are in their business.

I worked in the counseling field for fifteen years and worked part-time in my private practice for five years before I took the leap and went into full-time private practice. I honed my skills and learned tons about how to run a business in those five years. So, when I jumped to full-time, I felt in my soul that my business would grow, and I knew I would be ready for it. My business is not where I foresee it being just yet, but it is so close that I can feel it!

So, understand that your time will be sacrificed. You may not be able to attend every function, concert, or family event because you know there is too much work to do. That is ok. Keep in the forefront of your mind that your sacrifices today will allow you to live the life of your dreams and to create a bright and comfortable life for your loved ones in the future.

Money: Get ready to sacrifice your money! It takes money to make money! Those are sage words! You will have to spend your money in some way in order to create your products or to perfect your services. You will also have to spend money to set-up your business.

If you want to attract your ideal client and you want them to pay you top dollar for your products or services, then you will have to spend money. Plain and simple.

How you spend your money will determine the type of customer you will attract. If you are cheap and you try to sell cheap, low quality products for premium prices then you will lose customers. If you charge top dollar but know that you are not qualified to perform the service that you are promoting in your business, then you will lose customers. Period.

If you want to be a highly successful entrepreneur, you **MUST** give clients your best. Give them the best product or the best services that their money can buy. Now this is not to say that if you are starting out with a low budget that you have to go broke trying to give your customers the best of everything. Let's be reasonable here. However, take your time and do it right. If you don't have the money, take your time to create small batches of your product, save the money to feed back into your business, and don't officially launch your business until you are ready. Same thing applies to service-based businesses. If you cannot afford to provide a clean, comfortable, and professional environment for your customers, then wait, save your money, and then hang your shingle.

There is nothing worse than cheap products being sold at premium prices or a dirty, disorganized office space! That is my opinion and I'm sticking to it. Now, will some people still utilize your products and services? Yes. However, they will most likely not be the kind of customer you want, and they will probably haggle you about your prices because they know that you know it is overpriced and low quality.

Begin with the end in mind. If you want a great, long-lasting reputation in the community you work in then start GREAT. Doing so will make you a legend!

4.5 Branding Your Business

Now that we have that out of the way, let's start setting up your business. The first order of business is to come up with a name for your business. Will you use your name within the business name or do you want it to be a standalone entity?

Business Name: Choosing the name of your business is very important because in essence you are creating your brand. Your brand is the thing that will help others identify you.

If I say McDonalds, don't you immediately get an image of those golden arches in your mind? If I say Oprah Winfrey, don't you immediately get an image of her in your mind? Both of these are brands. It is that image that comes to mind when we talk about a particular person or place.

So, when you create your business name, be aware that this is how your business will be identified for years to come.

Logo: If you do not want to be the symbol for your business then you will need to create a logo. The logo should look professional and not be so deep that customers, who know nothing about your business, will have a hard time figuring out what you do. Simple and clear-cut is the way to go so that people can easily find you and utilize your products or services.

When I started my private mental health practice, I purchased my logo from Staples. It cost me $30 and was a puzzle with one piece missing. My concept for this logo was that I was the missing piece, so it worked perfectly until I found out that the missing puzzle piece was associated with people with Autism. That was not my target audience, so I had to revise the logo.

My current logo was created by a logo developer for a few hundred dollars. This seems expensive but big corporations often pay thousands of dollars for one logo so that price wasn't too steep when you think about it that way.

My current logo looks like a butterfly but when you look closer it is actually a man and a woman facing each other. Like my first logo, underneath the symbol I have my business name, Deirdre Haynes Counseling Services. The logo looks simple enough but if you look a little deeper you realize that the butterfly represents metamorphosis and the man and woman represent the population that I serve. They are head to head because there are problems. Most people don't think that deeply, but some do, and I did when I created this logo. My advice is that you should too.

Business Colors: When you are in the process of branding your business, think long and hard about the colors you will use to represent your business.

Most people simply use colors that they like. My favorite color is blue. So, I researched (remember R&D?) what the color blue symbolized to see if it would convey to my potential customer what my business was all about. Turns out that blue does represent water (flow/movement) and promotes relaxation. That was perfect! I want my clients to feel relaxed and yet I want them to feel that they are moving from where they are to where they want to be when they utilize my services.

So, before you jump off the deep end into an abyss of your favorite color, take a moment to see if it promotes the mindset that you want from customers that utilize your goods and services.

Think of the gym, Orange Theory, and ask yourself why they used so much orange in their logo and in their stores? It's because the color orange stimulates people and symbolizes energy. I'm sure that they put more thought into their name, logo, and colors but you get my drift.

4.6 Business Licenses

After you have named your business, created a logo, and decided on your business colors, it is now time to make your business a real entity. It is time to get your business license.

Many people that work from home creating their products tend to work under the table. What that means is that they don't get a business license, so the government does not know that they exist. This may seem cool but if you really want to create a "real business" that brings in the big bucks then you have to get licensed.

If you are running a business, then you will have to get a business license. The business license registers you as a legal business. This allows for you to obtain a tax identification number (TIN) and tax-free perks with stores, but it also puts you in position to be taxed by the federal and state government. This is not fun. Trust me. However, remember when I said you have to spend money to make money? Well, you can't become a million-dollar business owner and think that you won't have to pay taxes. It's not happening.

You need to get real clear right now on this. Would you rather pay $300,000 in taxes and make millions or do you want to not pay taxes and make $1000 a year in business proceeds? If you enjoy playing small, then do the latter. However, if you want to live the life of your dreams, which takes money, then you will have to sacrifice and pay the cost to be the boss!

So, I'm going to assume that you are tired of playing small and you are ready to get into the major leagues. That means that you need a **business license**. Most business licenses are relatively inexpensive. I have paid $150 a year for a license on one side of town and $80 a year for a license on the other side of town. I have heard of other people paying only $30 for their annual business license. Your fee will depend on the type of business you are opening and the area that your business is located in.

If you sell products, then you will also be required to get a **retail license**. This license tells the government that you have items to sell and they want their cut. The government gets their cut by taxing you.

How you will be taxed is based on how you structure your business. *I will not go into major detail about tax structuring because I am not a tax professional.* However, I will say that some of your options are to structure your business as a sole proprietorship, Limited Liability Company (LLC), or a Corporation. There are many other structures but those are the more common ones.

You can find out more about business licenses, retail licenses, and tax structures by visiting your local small business office and researching this information online.

4.7 Business Location

The next order of business is to decide on whether or not you want to run your business out of your home or if you need to secure a separate location.

If you have a product-based business, you could possibly create your product at home and then take it to other locations to sell such as fairs, flea markets, etc. If your business starts to gain a lot of momentum, most product-based business owners begin to run out of room to house all of their products as well as the materials needed to create their products. When this happens, you may have to consider moving to a **small retail space**. Examples of possible retail spaces range from storefronts all the way up to big box businesses like Walmart and Target.

Depending on your service-based business, you could also work from a home office instead of an office location when you start or even permanently. For example, if you have a web-based business where you create websites for other businesses, then your home office is probably sufficient since you won't have customers visiting your home. Some people opt to use their home even though customers may visit their house for services. For example, an accountant could opt to have people visit their home.

If you decide to get an outside office space, then you would most likely be looking for an **office space** to house your business. Offices vary in size and configuration depending on the design of the office building. Generally, you would enter one door to then access several offices that can span several floors.

Personally, I prefer to keep my home life and work life separate, so I pay for an office where I see my mental health clients. I use my home office for my online self-help store because all of my products are online in the form of books and courses and my customers don't have to visit my home to purchase my products.

Things To Consider: You can choose either option but make sure that you recognize that you are an actual business and no matter where your customers visit you, it needs to look and feel professional.

I will go into the idea of professionalism in an upcoming section, but I want to stress here that you need to make sure that you consider the **client experience** when choosing your location.

When I sought my counseling office I took note as to whether or not the location was in a high traffic area or not. Privacy is important to my clients and I wanted them to feel they could enter the building without everyone on the street knowing where they were headed. I also kept the idea of safety at the forefront of my mind as I sought a place to practice because I often work late, and I want my clients to feel safe coming to and leaving my practice. Of course, I want to feel safe as well.

Ask yourself these questions as you search for a suitable office space or retail space:

1. Is privacy and confidentiality needed for the clients/customers that utilize your products or services?
2. Will clients need a vehicle to see you or is your business conveniently located on a bus route or by other modes of transportation if they do not have a vehicle?
3. Does the retail or office space need to be in a high traffic or low traffic area?
4. Would a storefront space or an office space be more suitable for your business?
5. Is it ok for your business to be upstairs?
6. Is your office accessible for people with various disabilities?
7. Is the location of your office predominantly safe especially at night?
8. Is the area well-lit so that customers leaving your business will feel safe walking to their vehicle or waiting on transportation?
9. Do police officers patrol your business location or is security present?
10. Is the business located in the front or back of the building?

4.8 Business Forms

Now that you have decided on your business location, it is time to prepare for your customers by diving into the paperwork part of your business.

Every business has its own unique set of forms that are required to ensure that it runs effectively. Let's discuss some of the basic forms that your business will most likely utilize.

Receipts: One of the first forms you will need to create are your business receipts. Some people opt to use receipt books that can be purchased at office supply stores such as Staples. This type of receipt book works well for new businesses because the receipt books has the capacity to duplicate the receipt that you are writing on. You will need to keep a copy of the receipt to keep up with your gross sales and for tax purposes. **Remember:** You will not know how much money your business is grossing if you don't have an accounting method in place.

As your business grows, you will probably opt for a more professional and polished way to document your sales. I use Staples to create duplicate, full-page receipts that have my logo, contact information, and a brief description of the services rendered on it. I also have sections that allow me to write in my fees and the amount of the co-pays paid as well.

As you bill your clients, you will quickly figure out how your receipt needs to be set up in order to record this important information.

Invoices: As your business interacts with other businesses, you will soon learn about invoices.

When I hire someone to create products for my office such as banners and websites or to provide services such as painting or repairing something, they tend to send or give me an invoice. This invoice indicates what I agreed to pay them for and I am able to pay it at that time. Vice versa, if someone needs your services, then you will need to invoice (bill) them for your products or services.

There is a lot of software available that will not only allow you to create an invoice, but many will monitor whether or not you received payment, as well as send you reminders to ensure that you are paid. Square, QuickBooks, PayPal and many other online companies offer these services online. They also have the option to print it out and hand deliver it.

Estimates: A lot of businesses do not use an estimate forms, however, if you are providing a service that entails calculating the cost of labor and parts, then I believe that an estimate form is not only necessary but adds a professional touch.

Estimates also keep you from getting burned or jilted out of your hard-earned cash. Trust me I know! I have hired a business to complete multiple repairs at my office. When the owner did the walk through of my office space, I was promised the moon and the stars. I took a mental note of what was being offered for a premium amount and decided to hire them. Needless to say, over half of the job was not fulfilled and because I paid upfront, there was not much I could do about it. No estimate. No receipt. I was left holding the bag and doing most of the work myself! Lesson learned!

Trust does not belong in negotiations until you have worked with a particular company for a long enough period of time that you can determine their true character. I want to say that trust should never be utilized but admittedly some people run their businesses with integrity while others are simply trying to figure out a way to make a quick buck at your expense. The bottom line is that you have to protect yourself by having a paper trail in place. Estimates, invoices and receipts are the paper trail you need to ensure that the job gets done.

Having a system in place can save you a whole lot of headache in the future....TRUST ME!

4.9 It's Time To Get Paid!

Let's talk about your money honey! This is one of the best parts of owning your business. I say that it is ONE of the best parts of owning your own business because the very first part should be the rewarding feeling you get when you actually help someone with your products or services. Once you do that then you should feel incredibly proud and grateful that the products and services are providing a life and/or lifestyle that you can be proud of! You jumped in head first and people are responding to your business! Yes, you have every right to pat yourself on the shoulders! You rock!

Business Checking: Now that money is coming in, hopefully in droves, you have to be prepared to receive and keep up with the money. So, your first order of business, when you set up your business, should be to obtain a business checking account. You will probably need a business tax id number or your social security card (depending on your business structure) to open this account.

You will need to keep your business money separate from your personal money. You may pay yourself and your bills from your business income, but it needs to be kept separately for accounting purposes. To get more information about how to do this, please contact your local bank and/or an accountant.

Fees: You will also need to be very clear about what your fees are. I recommend that businesses create some type of pricing chart that they have in paper format or online so that customers know exactly what your fees are. This protects you because you can always refer them back to the pricing chart if they try to talk you down from your preset fees.

Having a pricing list also ensures that your customers know that you are not creating fees on the fly based on your current bills due, whether or not they can afford it, or for some other reason. There is nothing worse than having someone charge you an arm and a leg (and maybe a liver too!) for services that he or she may charge pennies for to someone that they know and or like. If this has ever happened to you then you know how you felt so don't do this to your customers or clients.

Have your pricing list posted or readily available so that your customer or client can make an informed decision about whether to utilize your services or not. If it is too rich for their blood or in other words they think it is overpriced, then you have to be willing to let them go. This is if you know in your heart that you have priced the item fairly.

Some business owners price gouge. That means that they jack the price up for items or services they know do not cost that much. This is a big no-no. You want to be fairly compensated for your products or services, but you also want it to be fairly priced.

A rule of thumb is to research other products or services in your area/niche that are similar to yours. You may opt to charge the same amount for your product or even a little less if you are just starting out.

When I initially opened my private practice and I was awaiting approval to bill various insurance companies, I charged clients $40 per hour since my clients were paying out of pocket. Once I was approved by the insurance boards and had more experience, training, and expertise under my belt, I moved my price to $100 per hour. Currently I am at $125 per hour and my private pay clients (no insurance) happily compensate me for my time and expertise.

Please note that I also did and still do pro bono counseling sessions for people that I know need my services but can't afford it and are uninsured. I tend to see 1-2 people a year in this fashion. It is my way of giving back.

The process of figuring out your pricing sweet spot may take some time and adjustments, but at the end of the day, you should want your customers to go home happy and you should still be able to pay your bills.

Industry Secret #1: Many people are unaware that there are researchers that study the buying habits of people. Customers are often tracked by their telephone numbers, store cards, and email addresses (online). This is why they encourage you to use these items. Ever looked on Amazon for something and then logged into Facebook to see that product being advertised? It is no coincidence!

Industry Secret #2: Another secret is that researchers have found that prices that end with the number 9 or the number 7 tend to motivate people to purchase that product. I am unsure why that is, but my hunch is that it seems as if you are saving. Instead of paying $10 for something you are paying $9.99. Yes, it is only a penny but for some reason it works.

Consider these secrets when you are creating your price list and thank me later!

Payment Methods: This section is **PARAMOUNT**!! Please pay close attention to what I am about to say......

Make it easy for your clients to find you and to pay you!

Did you see me drop the mic? I did! If you do not learn anything else after reading this entire book, please grasp this concept. Make it easy for clients to find your business and then make it easy for them to pay you.

You need to have multiple ways for people to pay you. Yes, cash is king. However, having online methods for payment is also king nowadays. There is nothing worse than liking a product you want to purchase, and the business owner can only accept cash. News flash! Most people don't carry cash around with them. I try to have some cash, but I mostly use my debit and credit cards to pay for everything. So, if you can't accept it then I can't pay you. I don't get the product I liked, and you lose out on guaranteed money. We both lose!

On the flip side, there is nothing better than someone that says they accept cash, credit, or they can bill you online with PayPal, Square, CashApp or some other online program. I love it! It means that they are prepared to receive my money for their products or services and I am ready to give it to them. We both win!

Now some people will think to themselves, "Well, I only cut grass." No matter what your business consists of, if you are getting paid for your services, then you need to have various means of payment. What happens when my lawn guy asks if I need my grass cut and I do but I am not at home to pay him? He doesn't cut the grass or get paid because I am not there to pay him in cash. This is detrimental to your business, no matter how big or small it is, and quite frankly it is unprofessional.

If you want to live the life of your dreams, then you have to wrap your mind around the fact that you are a professional. I know I have said this several times in this book, but it is just that important! Professionals behave in certain ways which is why they make the large amounts of money they make. Unprofessional people behave in certain ways and that is why they are often broke, have to close their business, and never seem to win. It begins in your mind. **Change your mind and change your life.**

Ok, I'm stepping down from my soapbox.

So, back to what I was saying, make sure you have multiple ways of getting paid. This applies to online businesses as well. Make your payment buttons clear and easy to find on your website. No one should have to hunt through all the pages on your site to figure out how to pay you money for your products or services. If they are like me, I move on to another site because I figure that they don't want my money since I can't figure out how to pay them. Moving on….

A word about checks: Personally, I no longer accept checks. Nowadays, most people pay with cash, debit, or credit anyway but another reason I don't accept checks is that I have been burned too many times. When a person writes you a check, you have no way of knowing if the account is even real. Some people have stolen checks or are writing checks off of an account that they know has been closed.

Once the check bounces, you will be responsible for paying your bank a fee for the reversed deposit. **Get this.... You have provided services and now you get the honor of not only paying the bank a fee, but you now have to hunt the perpetrator down to collect your money.** The majority of the time you will not get your money or see that person again.

So, accept checks at your own risk. You've been warned.

Part 5:

Professionalism

5.1: Professionalism

I would be remiss if I did not specifically address the issue of professionalism. Professionalism is not simply about how you look and/or dress, but it is so much deeper than that. You can be the most well-dressed person in the room and still not behave in a professional manner. Professionalism also includes your work ethics, character, and sense of integrity.

5.2 The _____ Experience

If you are a professional, when customers or clients experience you, they should feel like they have been in the hands of an expert. No matter what you do for a living. Clients seek the "experience" of being in your presence or of patronizing your business. This is the "thing" that they are willing or not willing to pay for…the experience.

When people pay hundreds of thousands of dollars to drive a Rolls Royce Wraith, a company that does not do any formal advertising by the way, they pay that money for the experience of that particular product. Rolls Royce has the reputation of being exclusive, luxurious, and it signifies that the person driving it has the money to comfortably pay for it. That is why you don't see a lot of them rolling through city streets.

The Rolls Royce Wraith owners are not only paying for a fabulous vehicle, but they are paying for the experience of driving it. They know that people that see them driving it will think of them in a particular way.

This concept also applies to handbags. Whether an expensive handbag to you is a Michael Kors or a Hermes Birkin handbag, at the end of the day, you have purchased (or desire to purchase) that handbag because of what it represents. Your business is no different.

All the previous sections have culminated into this very point. **When you start your business, you are creating an experience**. As I said earlier, for me, I like to call it the Deirdre Haynes Experience. Insert your name after the word "The" and before the word "experience" and figure out what that means for you.

When people enter my office, I want them to feel relaxed as they listen to classical music playing in the waiting room. I have paid top dollar for new, clean, and modern furniture in that room. I have a sectional with several pillows and a chaise lounge chair in there so that they immediately get the perception that I want them to feel safe, comfy, cozy and relaxed once they enter my office space.

My office is not always neat when I am in there working alone but during my office hours, my desk is clean and neat, and my paperwork is temporarily hidden in my file cabinets. I have a square debit card machine on my desk and receipts at my fingertips. When they enter the room to pay they know what to expect and they quickly exit to carry on with their day.

When they walk into my counseling room, I have a leather sectional in there that is also decorated with pillows and I have strategically placed boxes of tissue, if needed. I have a white noise machine for confidentiality and an incense burning. I love the scent of patchouli because it is said to induce feelings of calm and grounding.

Everything from my pictures, to my rugs, to my chairs, to my incense has been well-thought out and planned. I intentionally do the things that I do to ensure that my clients feel better when they walk out than when they walked in. When clients compliment me on the set-up of my office, I beam with pride because they are responding exactly how I wanted them to respond and it keeps them coming back for more.

Please keep in mind that when I started my private practice, I was in one room. One small room with no windows and my clients said the same thing that they say now. It does not matter what your budget or office space constraints are, you must keep your customers or client's needs in the forefront of your mind as you set-up your business. This will ensure that you have repeat customers and they will brag to their friends about your business which will inevitably bring in new business.

5.3   Have Your Stuff Together

As your customers or clients experience you, it is imperative to have your stuff together. What that means is that you must be organized. If you take the time to forecast your customer's needs and questions ahead of time, they will thank you with continued business later.

As the owner of your business, you need to know how it works. Yes, all parts of it. It is not enough to say that you will have to check with someone else unless you have a huge corporation. Doing so in a small business comes off as incompetence to the client. How will they know what to do if the owner doesn't even know what to do? Another lost sale!

So, have your forms in order. Have your prices and payment methods in order. Have your documentation of previous visits in order and be ready for any question that a customer asks. I went so far as to answer some frequently asked questions on my website. The end goal is to make utilizing your products and services as **convenient** as possible for the customer.

5.4   Under promise and Over Deliver

Please do not make promises you cannot keep! Let me say that again. **As a professional business owner, do not make promises that you cannot keep.** Whether you provide an invoice or not, which I advise you to do, make absolutely sure that **EVERYTHING** that you said you were going to do is done **AND** it is done in the time frame you promised.

Did you hear my heavy sigh? That is one of my personal pet peeves. People love to offer you the moon, stars, and some unknown planets when they are trying to make a sale. However, when it is go time, suddenly they fall flat. Suddenly, their dog died, their long-lost uncle died, their child was sick, their car didn't start, or they had to run to New Mexico to pick up a lost family member!

At the end of the day, **NO ONE CARES**! I know that sounds harsh, but this is business. People are relying on you to provide the service that you claimed you could provide. Now that you may have been or may not have been paid, suddenly you have every excuse in the book. **That business professional still has the same needs and the same deadlines they had prior to paying for your services. DON'T DO THIS**! This is a surefire way to lose business no matter how awesome you are at what you do!

This is why I say that you need to **under promise**. What that means is that if you think that you can finish all that is being asked of you in one week, then quote a two-week waiting period. That way, if you finish early you are the hero. If something really does come up, then you have given yourself additional time to get it done without stressing. Either way, you look professional in the eyes of the person that hired you. You have **over delivered** by delivering an excellent product early. Now you have a repeat customer and one that will brag to their friends about the awesome work you did. That my friend is what you want to happen.

I know several highly talented business owners that I refuse to mention or refer to other businesses because of their poor work ethic. I even gave one person the benefit of the doubt since they had a death in the family and their child was sick. However, to promise a one-week turn around and then take an additional three weeks to complete a project I was told I had to pre-pay for was absolutely ridiculous. There will not be a third time to disappoint me.

Was the final project pretty great? Yes. Will I rehire them or refer people to them? No. Don't be that guy or girl.

5.5: Be On Time

If you have a business that requires that you meet with customers or clients, then please ensure that you are on time. Your customer or client should not have to wait on you to pay you money. Let me say this one again…

Your client should not have to wait on you to pay you money.

Period.

You are providing a service to your customer or client. They are willingly paying you for that product or service. Don't let them down by having them wonder if you will even show up. That is bad business 101. If anything, you should be waiting on them, with a smile on your face, because each customer or client you have is paying another bill or allowing you to purchase something that you want. **They are a blessing, not a curse.** Please treat them as such.

I generally start seeing clients at 9:00 am or 10:00 am depending on the day. You can find me there around 7:00 am or 7:30 am. Why? Because I know that things can happen, so I allot time for happenstance. What if there is a train, or an accident, or I forget something and have to turn around? Starting out early allows me to handle those unpredictable things without inconveniencing my client.

Now of course, nothing in this world is fool-proof. Things will happen that you did not plan for and you simply will not be able to make it or make it there on time. **If that happens make sure you inform your client as soon as possible so that they do not come to your business looking for you and you are not there.** Not only is that embarrassing but it leaves a bad taste in your customer's mouth and they may not return.

A good rule of thumb is to imagine how you would feel in this instance or in any of the instances I have listed in previous sections. Would you like to be treated poorly? Would you like to be taken advantage of or be treated as if your business means nothing to the business owner? I am going to assume you would not like that and if you felt that way that would be the first and last day that you used their services. Your customers and clients feel the exact same way. Remember that.

5.6 Be Transparent and Honest

Now, I have been ranting in the previous sections because I can not stress those concepts enough. However, I know that sometimes things happen. Your beloved pet really does die, and you really did have to run to New Mexico to rescue a family member. When those things happen all, you can do is be truthful, inform the customer as soon as possible, and then try to make it right. Sometimes you still can't make it right but at least you can rest in the fact that you tried.

With that said, these mishaps should not occur every time you work with someone. If it does, then maybe you are not ready to be in business. Handle your personal issues first and then put yourself and your business back out there when you are really ready.

Not only should you be transparent about your ability to do things and get things done in a timely fashion, but you should also be transparent and honest with your products and services.

Don't sell people things that you know are defective, have been worn or used previously by others, isn't clean, or has unseen damages that you know about. Please don't do that to make a quick buck because it will probably be your last quick buck. Seriously!

If you want to be considered as an excellent business professional, then you must act like it at all times. Don't charge premium prices for subpar products and services. Don't come up with sneaky ways to make money under the table, thinking that you are getting over on the person buying your products or services. Don't get someone's money and dip.

All of those behaviors show people your **CHARACTER**. If you are doing these things, then please take a good long look in the mirror and tell me if you like what you see. When you do those things, you are setting yourself up for failure.

The same people that say they can't catch a break or are always broke are the very same people that do these types of underhanded things.

I'll let that soak in.

Now please tell me that I'm lying. I'll wait.

People that do those underhanded things are simply reaping what they have sown. **What goes around comes around**. It never ceases to amaze me that the people doing these things fail to see why things are not working in their favor. Duh! It's because of you. Call it karma or bad luck but when you have poor business practices it will eventually catch up with you.

Do unto others as you would have them do unto you.

The end.

Part 6:

Marketing Your Business

6.1 Marketing Your Business

Now that you have firmly established your business in the community or online, it is time to market your business. Marketing has changed over the years but there are important features in the historical and innovative methods of marketing.

Please note that a more detailed book is in development that will dive into the concept of marketing your business, so I will not delve deeply into those concepts here. Stay tuned!

6.2 Historical Marketing

Historically, business have advertised their business using traditional means such as newspapers, television, and radio announcements. These methods are still used but their exorbitant costs made it virtually impossible for small businesses to get air time and attention.

Business Cards: Business cards are another historical method of gaining attention that is still utilized today. When you are in the process of preparing your paper products (business forms) make sure that you create an attractive business card to give out at networking events and while you out and about during the day. You can have business cards printed at Staples, Vistaprint and other outlets that supply businesses.

Remember that your business card symbolizes your business so make sure that you get a quality looking business card. Include your contact information and your logo (optional) to make a lasting impression with your potential client or business associate.

Word of Mouth: Word of mouth has been and still is one of the most powerful tools that can make or break your business. If a person utilizes your products and services and they rave about how awesome it works or how professional, you were then you will definitely gain more business as a result of this act alone!

I have had one client tell four other people about me and all of them became a client of mine. From one person, I gained four more clients! Of course, I began to sweeten the deal for her by cutting her costs and to this day she and all four of her friends patronize my private practice and purchase my books.

Again, word of mouth can literally make or break your business. **Let me add that the lack of word of mouth can also break your business**. When someone doesn't perform as expected, I refuse to refer them to people I know. I refuse to have my name associated with someone that does not perform well. Others do the same thing and those actions will eventually slow and eventually break your business.

Will you have customers or clients that simply dislike you and your business for no reason? Yes. Prepare yourself for that. **However, if several people are saying the same negative thing or refuse to pass your information on to a colleague or friend because of your poor performance, then that tells the other person something about you**. So much so that when someone asks them about you, they will most likely repeat what someone told them, and the process continues until no one wants your business. Another business shut down before it had a real chance to grow.

6.3   Innovative Marketing

Times have changed and the methods that people use to market have moved online. Instead of paying astronomical amounts of money to advertise in traditional/historical ways, people have figured out how to advertise, mostly for free, online!

Social media outlets such as Facebook, Instagram, Twitter, Linked In, and Pinterest to name a few have changed how businesses get the word out about their products and services.

Someone that works from home can jump on a Facebook live and discuss the new body products they created. At the end of their demonstration, they can tell their viewers where to go to buy those products by posting a link to their website. Just like that, for free, they have made some sales, all from the comfort of their home!

Sometimes, people have jumped Facebook live to share a hobby such as applying makeup or styling their hair/wig. People that are watching all over the world may want that particular eye shadow or wig and they begin to ask where they can purchase it. Boom! Just like that a business has started!

My advice is to think outside the box when deciding on ways to advertise your business. I love the idea of advertising virtually for free. I also love the fact that people around the world could potentially purchase my products. The monetary potential is unlimited!

As I stated earlier, I am currently working on a book that will dive deep into these concepts and I plan to share all that I learned, and I am currently learning about online marketing.

Thank You!

This concludes our journey together. Thank you so much for purchasing **The Quick and Dirty Guide to Starting Your Business!** I pray that you gained some valuable nuggets of information and/or inspiration by reading this book. Now go out there and start that business!

Please check out some of these other books and workbooks written by Deirdre F. Haynes on Amazon and at other fine book retailers:

The Cheatsheet: Who Are You REALLY Dating?

The Quick and Dirty Guide to Overcoming Infidelity

Blindspots: Everything You Didn't Know You Needed To Know About Starting A Mental Health Practice

The Vault

The Vault: Anxiety Edition

The Vault: Depression Edition

The Vault: Gratitude Journal

The Vault: Group Therapy Edition

The Vault: Therapist's Edition

The Vault: Journal For Men

The Vault: Journal For Women

The Big Book Of Communications

www.ingramcontent.com/pod-product-compliance
Lightning Source LLC
Chambersburg PA
CBHW071433220526
45469CB00004B/1516